Halt 2 Proceed

Halt 2 Proceed

Alan Owen

First printing: 2019
This edition: 2021

ISBN-13: 978-1-9163314-0-2

British Cataloguing Publication Data:
A catalogue record of this book is available from
The British Library.

Also available for Kindle.

Contents

Acknowledgements

Many people have contributed to this edition of *Halt 2 Proceed.* They have influenced this book with their inputs, courses, leadership and knowledge, and the effect they have had on me during my life journey is unbelievable.

This edition was written following many reviews of the original edition of *Halt 2 Proceed* and discussions with people who read the book who were either retired or not able to work. It has been updated to include both personal and work aspects of life.

2020 was a difficult year for the entire world. Many enforced changes were put upon us, and many families lost loved ones to COVID-19.

It was a year in which I underwent several changes and it was personally very difficult, but special people who stood by me have made this new edition possible.

Thanks to the founders of LABRATS, who have journeyed with me, supported me unequivocally and provided praise and criticism where it was needed.

My team at ICARIS have been fantastic, giving me the time and space needed to complete this book. With so much going on in everyone's lives it was difficult to find quality time, but they enabled me to do this, especially Matthew

Jarvis, who has taken on the MD role.

To my wife, Melanie, who puts up with my ideas, jokes and rants and still loves me; and my son, who is always asking questions and ensuring that my feet are firmly placed on the ground. Without them, this book would never have been written.

And lastly to my dogs, who help me to escape day to day life. Walking in fields with three dogs gave me the time to reflect on and enhance this book. I know they cannot appreciate this, but time spent with them is invaluable.

Introduction

Halt 2 Proceed is a programme that enables people to stop and reflect on their lives and to move forward with greater purpose. It provides techniques that can be used across all aspects of life.

After implementing hundreds of systems over 25 years of working within an IT environment, the idea for the programme came when I was involved in an implementation that changed the way I looked at teams and how they interact.

For many years, we had implemented systems in the same way, developing software for the client with techniques to ensure the client received what they required. It was successful, but there was always resistance to change from the users of the systems, and the environment where we trained, developed and implemented was too regimental.

I was commissioned to provide a Case Management System to provide support for over 300 users in 50 locations across the UK that was intuitive and would reduce duplication of effort.

I started along my normal path of implementation, setting up meetings with the managers and providing an implementation timetable. When the client was presented with this, the director told me she did not want to implement they system as per my plan; she wanted to involve the support workers directly and set up a 'Thinking Culture', to allow for input from the users. This was to continue for the life of the project and would enable users to be empowered with the product and ensure the product continued to evolve.

I had always wanted to try out this type of implementation, as users always complained during training that they had never been consulted; the managers never understood what they did and they were never involved, or their opinions asked.

A working group was set up, with representatives from the user community at all levels and from every department in the group. We started by introducing the project and then asked them for their ideas on how they wanted the user interface to be designed, even down to the font size. We ensured that everyone had a chance to contribute, their opinions were documented, and decisions were made based on their input.

Obviously, we needed basic functionality of the software – it had a defined purpose – but how it was implemented and designed was the responsibility of the working group. The software was developed, installed and continues to be enhanced using this model today. Regular meetings with user representatives take place, their ideas and suggestions are all documented and implemented, and the software is in a 'fluid' state, with changes made every two weeks.

For anyone who is not in the software development arena, this is not the normal lifecycle of a piece of software. Release dates, patches and updates to versions are usually tightly controlled, with release cycles and an 'end of life' built into each piece of software.

This software implementation has been the most successful I have been involved in, due to the time and effort put in by everyone involved in its development. And it was this that led to the original Halt 2 Proceed programme being developed. Empowering employees and understanding the team environment and the interaction between people is the key to the programme.

This new edition takes those techniques and explores how individuals can use them to change their everyday lives. By following the steps in this book, situations can be managed differently, changes both large and small can be made, and all aspects of life, both personal and business related, can be analysed.

The programme has taken years to develop and draws on knowledge from several sources, including personal experience, and input from business leaders and from a board of trustees who have provided the final steps.

Clore Social Leadership enabled Halt 2 Proceed – both this book and the programme – to be completed. It was an idea that shaped many presentations, training courses and meetings, but had never been recorded. Now, for the first time, individuals can use these techniques for their own personal development.

Why We All Need to Halt

Everyone leads a busy life; there are pressures everywhere. Our world is a very noisy place with many distractions. It was once described as 'The Rat Race', but it is more than that now. Everything is instant, on-demand; society expects instant communication. The art of relaxing and taking solitude has disappeared.

On a tube journey to central London, I analysed the occupants of my carriage. Out of twenty passengers, only one person was not using a phone or tablet or reading a newspaper. That person just sat and observed everyone else. That person was me. Nobody spoke to anyone; they were all immersed in their own worlds, looking at emails, the news or playing games. Some were watching downloaded movies.

We all have an escape. The people watching movies, reading the news or playing games were escaping; they had their own solitude. Those who were checking emails or typing documents were not escaping, they were catching up, preparing for meetings; they were feeling the pressure of life.

It is almost impossible to escape in this 21st century on-demand society, with breaking news, social media, emails and the requirement to react instantly to situations all part of our world. Switching off and ignoring emails or messages from work when you are at home is very difficult.

Most of us now believe it is acceptable to answer work emails at home in the evening.

When I first started in IT and visited a client, I did not have a mobile phone. The protocol was to call the office when I arrived using the client's landline and then call the office again when I left. There was no further communication with the office. News was broadcast over the radio when I drove home. I had no idea what was going on in the office unless I was there. While I was with the client I would not know if a disaster had occurred in a foreign country, or even in the UK. I was isolated. I performed my job and went home, where I did not need to call my boss or dial in to systems to check messages. I did not even have an email address!

Now you may think this makes me a dinosaur; in fact, this was in 1992. IT systems were still implemented, and we still performed the same role we do today, but it was less noisy.

Think of the number of times you look at your mobile phone whilst reading this book, or the number of work emails you answer when you are not working. When you start to analyse and record this, it is frightening. I understand that our daily 9-5 has changed – some people work from home (especially during the pandemic), others have shift patterns, some are on call. But still, you need a work–life balance. If you do not look after yourself, how can you look after others?

Many people I have spoken to are retired or are caring for other individuals in their later stages of life. These people are still extremely busy, and their home life is impacted by their caring responsibilities. Whilst they are not working in a mainstream job, their caring responsibilities exceed that of a 9–5 job and the stress associated with these responsibilities is something that cannot be ignored.

My aunt, who is retired, tells me she has never been so busy, looking after grandchildren, meeting friends, attending dinner parties and travelling the world. She still has the stress of financial matters, ensuring that her bills are paid, juggling her time between herself and her children and grandchildren. This is another type of work–life balance and she still needs to make time for herself.

On airplanes, the safety briefing tells you that in an emergency where there's a lack of cabin pressure, oxygen masks will fall from the roof and if you have children you should put your mask on first, and then your child's. On a recent flight to America I wondered just how many people would do that?

It is the sensible thing to do – put your mask on first so you can look after others – but you wouldn't. You would put your children's masks on first, then yours, because your instinct is to look after them. And we do this – put other people before ourselves – in everyday life because of pressure from employers, children, partners and families.

For any parent, the merry-go-round of children's activities, school, holidays and sports is one that never seems to end, and balancing this with work and home is difficult. Add to the load a demanding workplace and a boss who expects you to work in the evenings, and the merry-go-round soon gets overloaded. Most people I speak to tell me they are tired and the tasks they face every day seem to get harder and harder. In addition, the external pressure of money is the main concern for many people today.

The pandemic has seen many people lose their jobs – the hospitality sector especially has been hit extremely hard – and financial responsibilities have become a major worry, with people asking, 'How am I going to pay the bills?' For those with children this is even more difficult, and keeping a roof over their heads becomes a full-time occupation.

Many people have lost loved ones during this pandemic or are now caring for people who are still recovering, and this has added an extra level of responsibility and burden to an already extremely busy schedule.

The main response I hear is 'I need this job; without the money, we would not survive,' and this is true. But how you manage the demands of the job can be changed.

I was struggling with two businesses, a charity, a sick 13-year-old son and maintaining a home. After discussing this with my Clore coach (Pat Joseph), we devised a plan of action and I halted, looked at what I was doing day to day and changed it. Not dramatically; I just empowered others by delegating responsibility and ensuring personal time was observed.

Halting and taking stock of the situation, looking at the areas I wanted to change and how I was going to achieve this, enabled me to re-adjust my work–life balance. We should all halt at certain times in our life – just stop, take stock and make brave decisions to change. There are some issues we believe are beyond our control, such as the pressure from managers to perform, but we are in control. We should not allow external pressures to affect our lives. We all need to halt. This is the only way we will proceed.

This second edition of Halt 2 Proceed will help you to stop, look at the situation and change aspects of your life so you can take time for yourself: time to recharge and to move forwards.

Hearsay – Too Much Noise

When was the last time you listened to hearsay? What did you do with the information? How did you act upon it? Would you say it was the correct decision?

The Halt 2 Proceed steps start with hearsay. We experience hearsay from a very young age. 'Don't play with Billy, he smells.' Sounds stupid, doesn't it, but we have all been conditioned by hearsay.

We have all made decisions based on hearsay. How many times has that decision been proved wrong? How many times have we trusted hearsay, only to find out that the hearsay is incorrect and the person who told you had their own personal agenda?

There is a lot of noise in the world today. We receive news all the time, direct to our devices, plus text messages, emails, social media feeds. Do we need to know that instant? Not really. There are always issues that affect us personally that we need to know about straight away – a sick relative, accidents etc. – but do these get mixed up in the noise of the world?

Social media plays a major part in most people's lives today, as we scroll through news feeds and read articles, posts and news stories. Do we spend too much time looking at articles that are not relevant to us? Of course we do.

SMS text messages for deliveries, appointments and

money-off offers are now commonplace. Five years ago, we didn't get reminders for dentist appointments; we remembered (or forgot) them. Why do we need them today? Have you ever thought why the organisations send out reminders? It is mainly for money: people who miss appointments cost money. A text message costs nothing compared to a missed appointment.

Everyone is after money-saving tips, 2-for-1 deals, discount codes, but being constantly bombarded with offers is noise we can ignore. But do we? Each time our phone vibrates or plays a tune, we look at it. We all do.

Social media takes up a lot of time in our already busy schedules. Some people escape to Facebook to look at funny videos, catch up with friends or just while away a few minutes whilst waiting for something else to happen (catching a train, for instance). Just how much information that we look at in those few minutes is important to us? Adverts tell us the latest multi-purpose cleaner will transform our lives, and we read and believe the comments, even though we have no idea who the people commenting are.

If someone came up to you in the street and said, 'You have to buy this kitchen cleaner, it is the best product ever made!' and would not move out of the way and you purposely had to move around them, you would be angry. You'd think, 'Why is this stranger in my personal space trying to sell me something I don't want?!' But then you go home, look at Facebook and think, 'That looks good, over 500 comments, I must buy it!'

When purchasing items online, many people read reviews on the product and then decide based on the reviews. These reviews are hearsay – they may be from people who have never used the product, have been paid to review the product or automated systems – yet we trust the hearsay.

In a business environment, we trust hearsay when listening to colleagues. The most common is 'They are a nightmare to work with. Good luck.' You are now thinking that a member of your new team is a nightmare; you have taken on board the hearsay. Did you ever stop to think that the person who told you may be the nightmare, and the person you are about to manage may be in need of support?

As children, we are all conditioned by our parents, teachers and friends. We support the football or rugby clubs our parents support. They influence our political affiliation, how we wear our clothes, hairstyles … In order to "fit in" we go with the hearsay; we follow the noise of the world. There are some that rebel, but most follow.

If you analyse the amount of hearsay you encounter in a week, you will be staggered. For instance, your sub-conscious will kick in when shopping. A new cleaning product has been advertised and your neighbour said it was good, so you buy it. Did you really need it? Why is it a necessity to buy it?

People are affected by hearsay from a young age. The child who was deemed smelly in primary school may turn into a great leader, but to those who knew him at school, he will always be "Smelly Billy". Hearsay conditions us, affects us every day and we must learn to stop listening to it, to make our own judgments based on facts. When you talk to Billy as an adult, you find out his mum left and Dad did not have enough money to buy a washing machine and washed everything by hand, so his clothes were often dirty. This was not a fault of Billy's, but the circumstance he found himself in. After discovering this, you now feel guilty for listening to the hearsay.

Stop for a minute today and think back to before you had a smartphone, before the internet and on-demand services. What did you spend your time doing? Did you have instant access to news from across the world before the internet? No – you only heard it on the scheduled TV or radio news broadcasts. Do you need to know it immediately today?

Some people love social media. They join groups that show pictures of times gone by, or groups for veterans, classmates and like-minded people. These are great for social interaction and to combat loneliness, but how much information do we really need? How much noise do we need to have in our lives?

If you are on a social media site such as Facebook, check your group memberships. How many times have you viewed the items in the group? Do you still need to be a member? I can guarantee there will be groups you have forgotten you joined.

Too often, our decision-making is clouded by hearsay. We use the noise to make decisions. They may not necessarily be the wrong decisions, but hearsay always plays a part.

Assumptions – Why Do We Assume?

I had the privilege of working under a fantastic manager; he was an exceptional boss, a brilliant man-manager. He told me: 'If you assume, it will make an ass out of you and me.'

This advice has stuck with me for 30 years. He was talking in the context of software development, where any assumption leads to unnecessary coding, extra time and delays implementing the solution. But this statement is true for all situations where we make assumptions.

On a very early training course that I was teaching, a participant stopped the course and asked me what a particular acronym meant. I had assumed the audience knew what I was talking about – I was using a basic acronym, with only three letters – but it had confused the participant.

This was a very important lesson to me as a young trainer. Why had I not put the meaning of the acronym on the slide? I knew what it meant, so I had assumed that, as the participants had signed up for the course, they would know as well. It taught me the very valuable lesson that you need to know the audience you are presenting to, and never use acronyms without an explanation.

I made a basic assumption, but often we combine hearsay with assumptions and draw our own conclusions, which are often based on the hearsay. Decisions are made with the assumption used as the main focus.

This was highlighted to me when I had finished a three-hour training session on GDPR (General Data Protection Regulation). The participants had engaged with the course and enjoyed it. One participant told me they had been dreading the course – three hours of boring data protection – but their assumption had been incorrect; they had enjoyed it and learnt from it and were very grateful to me for teaching them.

We all make assumptions, and many assumptions lead us to bad decisions. The worst assumptions are those made regarding people. People read articles and assume; they read reviews by other people and assume without the full facts of the situation. Some people even publicly comment without researching the situation and understanding it.

Involving people in your life with decision making and discussing issues with them can be hard, but it can also be rewarding. Every day, I read messages on social media sites and think: 'Why have they said that? If they had only talked to me, I could have informed them differently.'

Recently, I have been involved with a number of social media pages where comments are deleted when the owner of the page realises they have made incorrect assumptions that have been corrected by people within the group. Instead of acknowledging the mistake, the posts are just deleted. The person deleting the comments is assuming that other people in the group have not taken screenshots of the comments and that, by deleting the comments, the issue is resolved. This is false; you cannot assume.

A common statement is ‘I just assumed that you did not want to be involved. I did not want to disturb you; you are a very busy person.’ Assuming someone does not want to be involved in a decision-making process is an extremely bad decision. Many people want to engage but are never given the chance. People want to help; they want to be involved.

As people rise through the managerial hierarchy, the greater the assumption from their staff. The person at the bottom of the company structure will make lots of assumptions regarding the directors: ‘Why would they be interested in me? I am just the lowest of the low.’

I experienced the complete opposite when I went to work during my gap year from college. I was a student programmer, with no experience, yet during a team meeting, my manager asked me my opinion. I was shocked; I was 19, a student, and new to the business. He made me feel that my opinion mattered; he wanted to engage with me and know what I thought.

This made me feel part of the team. My input was minimal and had no effect on the project, but he had asked me. He had not assumed anything. Everyone had the opportunity to contribute.

Think of the assumptions you have made in life – how you have been influenced by hearsay or other people’s opinions, and why you assumed what you did. Think of the team of people you work with today or your circle of friends. How many assumptions have you made about them? How much have you listened to hearsay, assumed, only to find out the truth at a later stage? People have hidden agendas, vendettas against people, which they try to include you in.

How many times have you been told that someone did not like you or had said bad things about you, only to realise later that they had not said anything about you? They may have made assumptions about you, which are influenced by hearsay and other people's agendas.

I recently helped an elderly couple who had assumed that they could trust an old colleague with a very sensitive matter. Unfortunately that person was not to be trusted and he created a lot of stress, anguish and trouble for them; they made the wrong assumption. Yet they had a gut instinct not to trust him and they were right.

When I joined my first company, the managing director was the owner of the business and a very important person within the community. He had a very large house, a very successful company and commanded the attention of everyone when he walked into a room. I was in awe of him. I very quickly assumed that I could never talk to him; after all, I was a junior programmer with two levels of management above me before I could speak to him. I purposely did not engage with him out of fear for the first few months of my employment. I was the new employee, young, just qualified and had no real standing within the company. Then, during a summer event held at his house, he took the time to ask me how I was getting on and whether I had any concerns, and to say that his door was always open. My assumptions about him were completely wrong and it had affected how I interacted with him.

Think of the assumptions we make every day about how people dress for work, their punctuality, their body language; the boss who is unapproachable because of their position within the company. We do not know the struggles that people are going through daily. Someone who is experiencing major problems may be the happiest person when in company, but once alone, they suffer terribly. We never truly know a person. Everyone has secrets, everyone assumes, and we must try to stop the assumptions.

Most assumptions are made through fear or lack of confidence. The voice in your head that says you are not good enough. The fear factor. Removing assumptions is not an easy task – we all assume, every day. But to create a change in your life, you must remove the assumptions.

We build assumptions so we can justify situations, so we can avoid them or to make ourselves feel better. An assumption I hear all the time is 'My boss has never liked me.' After talking to the employee and the boss, this is false, 99% of the time; usually the boss just does not know how to handle the person.

'Why would they listen to me?' is another assumption. Most people we train consider themselves unimportant and not decision makers. They assume that they are not important. When you remind them that they are an integral cog in the system, and without them the system would not function, they start to remove some of the assumptions.

How many times have you thought, 'I could do that,' then never gone through with it? How many times have you assumed today? Look back at your assumptions. Write them down. How many are correct?

An assumption leads to bad decision-making. Remove the assumption, communicate issues honestly, and listen to each other. Sounds simple, but in a stressful environment, situations can easily escalate, and it becomes extremely difficult to implement this. But once assumptions are removed, the difference is incredible.

Change your philosophy. Think of a situation where you assumed. It may have been that a delivery was late, or a tradesperson did not turn up. What was your first thought? Was it that the person may have been involved in an accident, or may have suffered ill-health? Or was it that they were just incompetent?

If the delivery was late, how much did it impact on your life? Was it essential? Of course, there are times when it is essential to have a delivery on time (medicines etc.), but how many times is it really important that the latest delivery of a product ordered online turns up on time?

During this pandemic, many more people are ordering online than usual and the delivery and postal services are at breaking point. My brother-in-law is a postman, and he is working extremely long hours to ensure the post is delivered on time. But what about the impact on his life, his family? Is he missing out on social occasions?

What about care workers, doctors, nurses, emergency

services, shopkeepers, and all the other essential workers who continue to ensure the country keeps running – just how close are they to breaking point?

When we or a loved one must visit hospital for treatment, how much do we assume? Do we think about the nurse who is 11 hours into a 12-hour shift, whose feet hurt, whose stomach is growling because they did not get a lunch break? Do we consider that they may be thinking about paying the rent or the mortgage, have sick loved ones themselves or be recently bereaved? We do not know what they are going through. Everyone is fighting their own personal battles.

We all make assumptions, it is part of our everyday lives, but we can minimise them. Think before you post on social media. Think about the other person and what they are going through.

If you are relying on an assumption, do not act on it. Communicate, talk to the person, and remove the assumption.

Listen – Do We Do Enough?

In our Hearsay section, we discussed that we listen to too much hearsay. When we listen, do we listen actively, or just listen? I have attended training courses and presentations where, at the end, I cannot remember the presenter's name. I heard it, but I did not remember it. They told me, but I decided that it was not important at the time, as I was thinking about what to have for dinner.

We have all sat through conversations with bosses, friends and loved ones where our mind has wandered off, thinking about other things. We are still listening, but it is not active listening. Boring subjects, boring presenters, subjects we do not understand all make our mind wander.

My grandmother used to say that my grandfather had "selective hearing" and only heard what he wanted to. We used to laugh at her, but she was right. His mind had moved onto other thoughts. He was still listening, just not in an active way.

Our mind is always thinking, processing information that comes from all around our body. Listening is just one job it does. We use a unique combination of our senses when we listen. We use our sight, our hearing, and our sense of smell.

If a presenter is well dressed and attractive, we will instantly take notice of them and be interested in what they are saying. The subject may be boring, and we may switch off during the presentation, but the initial reaction was one of interest.

Interest in a presenter or a subject always promotes active listening. But when you must attend a meeting in which you do not have an interest, active listening is difficult as we have already assumed the meeting will be of no relevance. We all attend meetings in our daily lives: financial meetings, business meetings, personal meetings and meetings with our loved ones.

Think about how many times you have switched off over the last few days, when your mind has wandered onto other topics. Maybe you watched a TV programme and did not take in the plot. For drivers, we have all experienced driving down a road and not remembering it; we were in "auto-pilot" mode.

An ex-colleague now works for a multi-national company, working from home and regularly attending Skype meetings. He was invited to a meeting that had no video link, only audio. As he was at home, he made a cup of tea, sat down at his computer, and joined the meeting.

The meeting started and discussions began, but he was not asked for an opinion or to confirm he was even present. During the initial conversation, he started to wonder why he was there. The team were discussing a new project. He had no idea what the project was and, on checking the attendee list, he did not recognise anyone.

He checked the employee list online and found that there was another employee with the same name as him. He persisted with the meeting until one of the attendees asked him for his opinion. He then spoke up and pointed out they had invited the wrong person. Obviously if this was a face-to-face meeting, the problem would have not occurred. I asked him how long it took him to realise he was at the wrong meeting. He said it took around five minutes.

Interestingly, the person who should have been there did not raise any concerns about a team meeting he had not been invited to.

Listening to anyone, whether one to one or within a meeting, is a skill. This skill is not taught at school, despite us being expected to sit, listen, and learn. For many meetings where there is no interaction, participants are expected to listen to presenters for hours. Active listening in this environment is a difficult task.

We all have a "gut instinct", the voice in our head that we listen to every day. Sometimes we regret not listening to it. Sometimes it leads to assumptions. We hear this voice every day, but we need to ensure that when it is needed, we listen actively.

Distinguishing between everyday noise and things that need our attention is difficult. We experience noise from the minute we wake up until we go to sleep at night. So much is going on in our lives that we need to filter out the hearsay, the background noise and listen actively to what is important.

When was the last time you were in a one to one session and just sat and listened to the other person? We are all guilty of finishing someone's sentence, jumping into a conversation, when we need to just listen and allow the person who is communicating to finish.

This is a difficult skill to master. Everyone is so busy but taking time to just stop and listen is possible, though many of us believe it is not.

When a person is listening actively, their body language shows they are engaged; when they are listening passively, their body language gives it away.

I have attended many lectures where people were tired and uninterested, and you can tell they are not listening just by looking at them and their body language. They are there in body, but not in mind. Listening to the things that matter in our lives in an active manner not only benefits us, but benefits the person communicating with us.

A friend was contemplating giving up teaching as he was not receiving any interaction from his students. He was demoralized. 'Nobody pays attention in my lectures,' he told me. I asked the students why they were not paying attention and they said the lectures were boring and the teacher never asked for interaction; he just stood at the front and talked for an hour at a time. The students dreaded his lectures and new students were immediately told how boring they were. He had a reputation amongst the students for being boring and immediately they did not engage with him.

When I told him, he decided to change the way he communicated with his students. He provided an interactive subject for the students to raise their attention levels and they participated more. He involved them and actively listened to them. He had not listened to them before; he just taught them.

After a few lectures, I spoke to the students and they were very positive about his new approach. By interacting and actively listening to the students, he had developed a bond between them, and they had responded accordingly.

Just because you may be the presenter or the head of the family or a manager of a team does not mean you can stop listening. You need to listen to friends, family members and employees and engage them in your subject. Listening is a key part of everyone's life. You do it sub-consciously.

For some, listening is impossible. Deaf people cannot listen, but they communicate using other means, like sign language and lip reading. They actively focus as they need to concentrate on what is being said every time someone communicates with them.

I have worked with several deaf people and they are the best listeners. This may sound stupid, but they actively listen. They do not experience the white noise around them, the distractions of other sources. We need to listen when it matters. Everyone can benefit from active listening.

Actively listening to another person's point of view, their issues or their problems is a difficult task to master. Try it! Do not finish the other person's sentence. Let them pause; let them finish their point. Concentrate on what they are saying to you. Do not make any assumptions, or let your mind wander onto other subjects.

Listen to the other person, wait for them to finish, and then respond. You will be amazed by how difficult this is if you have an active mind or you are worrying about other things (financial problems, tasks, issues at work, issues at home) because they will pop into your mind.

The mind is a powerful tool. It stores and processes so much information every day. Harness the power of your mind and use it as a tool for active learning.

Our memories will also interfere with active listening sessions. Maybe there's a smell, a place or a song that was a favourite of a loved one who has died; an anniversary, a special day – these thoughts and memories appear at random times during the day. They are what makes us who we are; they are the result of our lifetime of experiences.

We can use these experiences to help people, but we must do so in an active listening manner. Try to avoid 'If I was you' sentences; instead say: 'Have you considered this scenario?'

Think – Do We Overthink?

As well as listening, we think constantly. Our mind does not switch off. Our body is a machine, and our mind controls every aspect of our being.

We think about situations and we make assumptions. Sometimes overthinking can be our downfall, but when should we think and when is it time to stop?

When we are presented with a difficult situation or something that upsets us or makes us angry, we think about it constantly. Issues that affect our everyday lives, such as money, children, partners, and work, all play a part in our daily thinking.

Sometimes the pressure of work makes us overthink; for instance, a mistake that was made which has led to a meeting that is yet to take place. We think the worst. We worry about the meeting and what is going to happen: will I be sacked, what I am going to do for money, how am I going to cope? It spirals out of control.

If we take time to stop and think, things are usually not as bad as we fear. By thinking too much, we create assumptions and fears that are unfounded. 'What if this happens?' is a common thought.

When was the last time you sat down and thought about your life, your work, your family, and any situations that you find yourself in (debt / relationships etc.)?

Think back to a situation you thought was hopeless – a project that failed, a car that broke down, a relationship that ended. Did you overthink it? Did you fear the worst? Yet you are still here.

There are obviously occasions – bereavement, for instance – that we will think about always. The loss of a loved one is a difficult time for anyone. We never stop thinking about the loss; we remember them always and at unexpected moments. There may be a smell, or a place, and we will be reminded of our loved one.

Controlling our thoughts can be difficult. We are all placed in situations we do not want to be in. We just need to learn not to overthink and create assumptions.

I found myself in such a situation when a former colleague sent me a letter from a solicitor demanding money for defamation of character. Immediately, my anger rose, and my mind went to the event (which had happened over 10 months prior). I began thinking about it and after the initial shock, consulted a solicitor who told me he would respond, and that the allegation was unfounded and would not stand up in court. I was relieved but continued to think about it. For the next few months, it was in my thoughts, but I did not overthink it. I did not make any assumptions or retaliate; instead, I listened to the expert, who gave me fantastic professional advice. Nothing came of the claim.

I did not let the situation affect my work. It was a distraction – and a large one at the time – but by not overthinking and actively listening to my solicitor, it did not need any of my attention. I could concentrate on more important things.

It was after this incident that I took time to think about my life and how I could change it for the better. By stopping, removing the assumptions I had built up, listening to the correct people and thinking, I adjusted my work–life balance and felt much better than I had in years.

Hearsay, Assumptions, Listening and Thinking (HALT). Many of us use some of these techniques in our lives already, but by combining them, honing the techniques and changing small aspects of our lives, we can improve our quality of life, de-stress and relax.

The Importance of Self-Reflection

During the Clore Emerging Leader course in 2019, I was introduced to the importance of self-reflection. This is the idea that we should take time to reflect on what we have achieved, what is happening in our lives and what is important to us.

After several coaching and active learning sessions, self-reflection has now become an important part of my daily routine. I take time to just sit and reflect on my day: what happened, how I coped, what I could have done better, and how I could have handled things differently.

This was something that I had never taken the time to do. We all need to reflect, and by halting, we can reflect on what has happened and what is happening in our life. By combining the techniques and taking a small amount of time to reflect, you can ensure that you are ready for the next step and move forward.

I often ask people if, once they have reflected on a situation themselves, they ask other people involved if they have also reflected on the situation and, if so, had they come to the same conclusion.

Reflecting as a group is also very important. Why did situations occur? How were they handled? How could the situation have been handled in a better way? What were the mistakes and, more importantly, what did we do well?

We normally only reflect on the bad things that happen: why did the project fail? Why did we not meet the deadline? But we must learn to reflect on the positive aspects, too.

In Nancy Kline's book *Time to Think*, she introduces a "Thinking Environment", where each member of the team is given an opportunity to discuss a positive thing that has happened to them. It does not have to be life-changing; just something that has gone well within the team. In regular team meetings, this does not happen. The manager normally dictates the agenda and only invites comments from certain people in the team. Some do not even contribute.

By self-reflecting and reflecting as a group, we learn to understand and appreciate each other, and we learn from each other and ourselves. We have all sent an email and then, 24 hours later, thought, 'Did I really write that!' It is important to sometimes HALT, reflect and then send the email.

By using the HALT technique in everything we do, we can reflect before proceeding. Our emotions can always get the better of us – anger especially, as we often conflict with other people. If we were to HALT and reflect on the situation, we would handle most situations differently.

I am often told: 'I do not have time for that, do you know how busy I am!' When I sit down with someone and analyse their workload, pressures and assumptions, everyone has time. Empowering others and reducing workloads, reducing the pressure, leads to time being generated.

Some of the best ideas have come when self-reflecting and discussing ideas with other people. The simplest ideas are the best ones. Steve Jobs of Apple combined an MP3 player with a mobile telephone and created the biggest invention of the 21st century, the smartphone. It was a simple idea with a simple interface, and it worked. He worked tirelessly for the company and became extremely wealthy. However, before his death in 2011, aged 56, he said:

'Remembering that I'll be dead soon is the most important tool I've ever encountered to help me make the big choices in life.'

and:

'Being the richest man in the cemetery doesn't matter to me... Going to bed at night saying we've done something wonderful... that's what matters to me.'

Unfortunately for Steve Jobs, it took terminal cancer for him to reflect on his life and to realise that the most important things were not material and despite his wealth he could not prevent his death. It is the ultimate self-reflection. He achieved so much in his life – he was an inspiration for others, a driving force – yet his dying wish was for life.

We all should take time for reflection every day before it is too late. Use this time to self-reflect and discuss it as a group with other people who were involved. We all make good and bad decisions every day. Take time to reflect on these decisions and learn from them. Make time. You will see the benefits.

What is Needed to Proceed

The HALT principle can be applied to any situation to remove the hearsay, the assumptions, take time to listen actively and to think.

We should use HALT constantly before we proceed and move forward. Before we can proceed, we must ensure that we are ready to handle the situation.

We must answer the following questions before we move forward:

P - Are you Prepared?

R - Have you Researched the situation?

O - Are you Organised?

C - Do you have the Courage?

E - Do you have the Energy?

E - Do you have Enthusiasm?

D - How much Dedication is needed?

Unfortunately, due to pressures of time, we are very rarely prepared to proceed. Many of us have attended meetings at short notice or that we have forgotten about and are not fully prepared. In these cases, we often lie to ensure we are not seen as being unprepared.

We do not want to seem as if we do not know what we are doing, that we are unorganised and cannot perform our job, so we cover up. Instead of telling the manager we were not prepared, we attend the meeting and hope we will not be asked any specific questions.

Being truthful with ourselves and our colleagues enables the whole group to perform in a more efficient way. Often situations will be treated in a different way and the outcome of the meeting will be completely different if everyone has an input and everyone is truthful.

We can use this technique in our home life, too. We all have deadlines, we all have tasks, and we all forget them at some point. By why do we forget the tasks? Do we Halt and think why?

Saying 'I am not ready to proceed' is often seen to be a weakness. Many people will continue to work under tremendous pressure rather than using the HALT principle. Unfortunately, this is usually down to the pressure exerted on them by their situation (it could be a partner, family matters or a job). Everyone is under pressure to deliver and this leads to a strained, stressed environment.

By communicating with everyone, and looking at the issues, the problems and the positives, the situation can be managed. There is always help available for any situation.

I was involved in a project that had stalled because of a lack of input from the client. At a meeting, the developers discussed an onsite discussion that had gone badly; the client was blaming the supplier and the supplier blaming the client. The HALT principle was applied, and the situation was discussed directly with the client. Specific contacts were identified who were to manage the project at both the client and supplier ends. Once this was implemented, the project was delivered on time and both parties were happy with the solution.

During the meeting, there was discussion about the difficulties of working together and the issues involved, and even a consideration of withdrawing from the project altogether. There was a lot of emotion, anger, and assumptions. Once these were removed the project continued, but without the HALT principle, the outcome would have been completely different.

We all find ourselves in situations where we do not want to be; this may be of our own doing or through the actions of someone else. Taking the time to deal with the situation correctly and removing the assumptions and the emotions will help the situation to be resolved.

Do not be afraid to say, 'I am not ready.' It is not a weakness, it is a strength. If you need help, ask for it. I am very involved in an organisation that works with veterans of nuclear testing and I have helped hundreds of atomic veterans and their families across the world, but I did not do this alone. There are fantastic people within the atomic community who have all helped solve problems and issues. We work as a community for a common cause.

Are You Prepared?

Preparation is key to ensuring any situation can be handled correctly. It is not just self-preparation; group preparation is often overlooked.

I once attended a meeting where an important decision needed to be made regarding a large investment of over £5 million. The board were expected to decide within five minutes of the agenda item. The chairman had prepared the item, but he had not prepared the board.

This led to a heated discussion regarding the investment and a decision was made to defer the investment until the next meeting, much to the annoyance of the chairman. This was not a decision that could be made without the correct preparation.

Time is the major factor affecting preparation. My manager once told me, 'To fail to prepare is to prepare to fail,' and he was right. When attending presentations, he knew the audience he was presenting to, the financial aspects, and the decision makers, and he ensured that everyone received pre-presentation documentation.

His presentations were always a success because he had prepared properly. I never saw him fail. He ensured that his preparations led to smooth presentations and never assumed anything.

In Lord Baden-Powell's handbook *Scouting for Boys*, the

scout motto is:

BE PREPARED

which means you are always in a state of readiness, in mind and body, to do your duty.

Key to this is that you are ready **in mind and body**. Just attending a presentation or a meeting in body, but then not listening to anything and not interacting, is not being prepared.

Unfortunately, many of us are not prepared. People tell me they are unorganised, always preparing things at the last minute and always rushing. Being unorganised leads to being unprepared. Using the HALT principle to organise your time and your to-do list gives you more time for preparation.

Using this technique within family life is very beneficial. Most tasks happen on a cyclical basis – school terms, bin collection, bill payments, eye tests, dental checks, shopping, for example. Being prepared is simply a case of ensuring you have reminders set. We live in a technological age of smartphones, smart watches, computers, Alexa, Google Home and many more gadgets that can help us to remember. If you can, use these gadgets to help you or write reminders in diaries. Take 10 minutes every day to prepare for the next day and check for any upcoming events. It sounds simple, but making changes like this can be difficult for some people.

We may not want to face some situations, we may be afraid

– of losing our jobs, receiving bad news, facing the consequences of our actions – we overthink things and always think the worst, but if you prepare correctly and take the time, you will be able to handle everything more effectively.

Saying 'I am not prepared' is one of the most difficult statements for anyone to make. It is seen as a weakness. Pressures exerted on us from external sources affect our performance; they affect our lives. As managers, we must learn to interact with our teams, interact with our managers and discuss situations honestly and truthfully.

Ensuring everyone involved in a project or decision is prepared and informed is the key to moving forward after halting. Without preparation, we cannot move forward. In the HALT step, we have removed the assumptions, listened, and thought, but now preparation is key. Preparation allows you to take the first step forward.

A car body-shop manager, who repairs cars after accidents, told me their job was 75% preparation and 25% finishing. Without anything less, the repair would fail, the finish would not be acceptable, and the car would not pass final inspection. Preparation was key to success.

We all come across situations that are beyond our control. It may be the death of a loved one, an illness or an incident such as a car crash. These are unseen events that we do not have time to prepare for. However, after these situations happen we can take time to prepare for the actions that follow, take time for ourselves and to process the information we have received.

I experienced this with the death of my father and my brother when I was in my early twenties. I was working in London when a colleague told me he had received a telephone call and that my brother had suffered a fatal heart attack. I needed to drive from London to Cheltenham to be with my family.

But before I drove back, my colleague sat down with me and made sure I was able to make the journey and that I was in a fit state of mind. He prepared me for the journey, which would take a few hours, during which time I would be alone.

I am forever grateful to Mr Mike White for the time he took with me during that day; he prepared me for what was to come. The organisation I was working for were fantastic and told me to go home and come back to the project when I was ready.

The journey home was a difficult one, but I was prepared to make it. There was nothing I could do about the outcome so I had not rushed into the car and set off immediately. The last thing my mother needed was for me to crash the car, speeding home.

If you are able, ensure you take the time to prepare, and ensure you have everything you need for the task.

If you are not prepared, do not take the next step forward. You will fail without the correct preparation. Take the time to prepare.

Have You Researched?

Research is the most important aspect of preparation. We all perform research every day, mostly financial research. When we receive our car insurance renewal, we research for the best price.

But do we research enough? When entering a project or a meeting with someone we have not met before, do we research the person? Do we know their background, their career, their achievements?

In this digital world, research is easier than it was 10 years ago. Do you know enough about your circle of friends or your work colleagues?

Research may be difficult but can provide insights into situations that would not otherwise be divulged. I was involved in an implementation of a new computer system; the suppliers were narrowed down to two, and one was chosen. We were contacted by the other supplier, who offered to implement the system for 50% of their initial quotation.

After researching the company and its financial situation, we found they desperately needed the order to keep the company afloat. They went into administration within a month of the decision.

There are different types of research, and information can be retrieved from many sources, some of which may not be relevant to the situation. However, each situation needs research.

I was asked by a colleague to research why an outstanding employee's performance had suddenly taken a downward turn: they were arriving late for work and falling behind with their tasks. Online research discovered they had recently suffered a relationship breakdown which they did not want to disclose. This research led to the manager approaching the situation completely differently. They discussed the situation, and the employee was given extra time and some of her tasks allocated to other team members.

On returning to work, the employee's performance returned to her usual high standards and she remained in position and achieved promotion. Without the research, the outcome may have been different.

We did not rely on hearsay: there were greatly differing rumours. By researching a situation and relying on information, you can move forward.

My sales manager would not make a sales pitch without researching every person attending his presentation. He ensured that he researched their background and their decision-making authority and would amend his presentation accordingly. He was very successful.

When attending a meeting where decisions need to be made, have you researched your position? Is the decision you make the correct one? Do you have all the facts?

When making financial decisions, the pressure put upon us

to decide can be enormous. You may be desperate; you may need to pay bills immediately, be receiving threatening letters and be under the threat of eviction.

These situations are extremely challenging for anyone to deal with, especially in the current climate, when people have lost their jobs, their livelihoods, and all sources of income.

However, researching the situation can help. There are many organisations that will help you, so get advice from experts and take the time to look at the options. A quick fix is not necessarily the right fix.

Do not ignore any letters that are sent and do not leave it until it is too late. Tackle the issues immediately. My father always worked on the philosophy that if we could not afford it, then we did not have it. Nothing on credit. This may seem old-fashioned, but he was right; there was no need for expensive purchases that would put the family in debt. Ensure you have a roof over your head, you can pay the bills and feed the family. Anything else is a bonus.

Many people are struggling to ensure the basic needs of their families today, but help is available from many sources, such as charities, governments, and Community Interest Groups across the world. Do your research, join community groups, ask for assistance. Do not bury your head in the sand. There are always people willing to help.

It saddens me every day when I hear that people have taken their own lives because they cannot cope. They struggle with their own problems and feel that the only way out is to not exist. It is heart-breaking for the people left behind – and it happens to people of all ages. We have all found ourselves in situations where we feel as if the world is against us, that nothing is going right, and we have no one to turn to.

But there are always people who will help you. I work with many charities who provide excellent services, from financial assistance to help with domestic abuse. These organisations provide life-changing services; they are making a difference.

We must understand that we are in control of our lives and we can use the research step to look into new worlds and new opportunities or perhaps to change our whole future. If we have time to volunteer, why not research the opportunities available? Our time is the greatest gift we can give and our talents can be extremely useful to other people and organisations.

Many people are happy with their lives but have always had a dream. You can realise that dream by researching the opportunities available to you and looking for help and guidance across the world, because people will always help and advise you.

Researching can also be a great way to relax and unwind, for example researching a new hobby or an area that you want to move into, getting involved in groups or forums, and watching videos on different topics.

Whether we are researching potential job opportunities, voluntary work or leisure activities, we can all use research to enhance our lives and it can be a positive step to a better future.

Everyone has different problems at different stages of life, and research is always a useful strategy. Find time to research your particular situation and find help. You are never alone.

Are You Organised?

When did you last attend a meeting where you were fully organised? We have all attended meetings where we are not organised, did not have the correct documentation, had not looked at the required papers.

We have all forgotten meetings and tried to prepare at the last minute. In every meeting, there is always at least one person who is not organised. The person who does not have the right paperwork, the person who forgot about the meeting until the last minute. But why does this happen?

We all have a work colleague with hundreds of icons on their computer screen: we look at them and say, 'How can you work like this?' but they do, and they know where everything is. But for some people, organisation is difficult to master.

Organisational skills can be learned, but for most people organisation harks back to their school days and how they were taught.

My English teacher made me write my name and the date at the top of every piece of paper and that is something I still do 33 years later!

Some people love organising with folders, colour-coded charts, different colour pens etc. But for others, it is not so easy. Some people see it as admin, and it is always bottom of the task list – especially filing.

When we teach organisation skills, we discuss how organised people are across their entire lives, not just in the workplace. Do they pay their bills by direct debit, keep receipts, have a diary, keep a calendar at home?

From this, you can build up the type of person they are. Some people seem to be disorganised but are in fact very organised within their own system.

When filing items, my wife files under references I would not use. For instance, the car file does not go under "Car", it's filed under the current model; "Mini", for instance. She instantly goes to this file when looking for any car-related paperwork, but I go to "Car" first.

Everyone is different and organises in a different way, perhaps by writing everything down, making to-do lists or keeping a diary / calendar.

When it comes to managing your time, a family, or a workplace team, it is essential you are organised. A meeting that takes place when the team are not organised is a meeting that will fail. How many times have you heard, 'Don't worry, we'll wing it!'

When preparing for a workplace meeting, make a list of attendees and the agenda, and against each item list the documents that are needed. If they are being prepared by another member of the team, ensure well in advance that they are still able to do this.

If you are preparing for a meeting regarding a personal situation, such as financial or with an organisation who you have reached out to for help, ensure you have what they need. If they have asked for three months' bank statements, have them to hand, as well as any correspondence from them relating to your situation.

So much time is wasted by organisations who are trying to help people with follow up letters and telephone calls when the applicant does not supply the correct information. Take the time to prepare and organise what is needed.

Sounds easy, doesn't it – but it isn't. Pressures of work and home often lead to items being forgotten or miscommunication about who does what. Ensure that team members' responsibilities are clear and make diary entries before the meeting to be sure that everything has been prepared. Do not wait until 15 minutes before the meeting when the diary reminder pops up and then try to collate the information needed. This will lead to an unproductive meeting.

We all get called to emergency meetings, where there is no time to plan or prepare, but in these circumstances, make it clear to the attendees what is going to be discussed and what is required of them. If possible, send documents to the attendees in advance of the meeting so they can prepare and organise their own schedules.

I was once told you could tell what type of person a colleague was by looking at their desk and working environment, and analysing the paperwork on their desk, the desktop icons, how much filing is in the out tray etc.

This does give an insight into the person's organisational

skills, but there are other factors to be taken into consideration. For instance, a managing director may have a personal assistant who organises all calls, ensures documents are ready, briefs them before meetings, takes care of their diary and ensures that filing is completed.

For some, the task of filing brings on a sense of dread. I am one of those people. Filing is boring, and it always seems as if there is a large pile of filing to complete. I feel like filing is not the best use of my time and there are always more important things to do.

But consider how much time is spent looking for documents when they are needed. For example, I was looking for a certificate I needed for me to enrol in a Masters' degree. I spent two days looking for the certificate. My wife has a folder for all her certificates, and she found hers in 10 seconds.

I did eventually find the certificate, but how much time had I wasted? A lot more than if I had filed the certificate correctly.

Organisation is key to ensuring that meetings run smoothly, required information is presented, people who need to attend the meeting are aware of their responsibilities and that the meeting is clearly defined in its purpose. You will save yourself time by organising your affairs, keeping documentation, preparing for any meetings and ensuring that the correct information is provided to anyone who is trying to help you.

Do You Have the Courage?

Courage – the courage to stand up in front of a room full of people and present – is not something we all have. It is something I hear all the time: 'I do not have the courage; I don't know how you do it.'

Courage is defined as '*the ability to do something that frightens one; bravery'*. People do not often say that they are frightened, more that they dread the situation.

I was once asked to present to over 600 people on a subject that I knew little about. I was very young, and I was frightened. Once my manager had given me the task, I could not concentrate on anything else. It occupied every moment of my thoughts, especially thinking about everything that could go wrong.

I researched the presentation, and I was organised, yet I was dreading it. I had never presented to so many people before. Then the owner of the company came over to me and said, 'You will do a great job. Just concentrate on your preparation and not on the crowd. Many are only here for a day off work and the free food!'

I laughed with him and immediately felt relaxed. These people were not here specifically to listen to my small presentation; they were here for several reasons, including the food.

The time came for my speech. I stood up and my

presentation was over in a blur. I received a round of applause and sat down again. I had overcome my fears.

Later that year, I met with one of the attendees of the conference and he told me he remembered my presentation, not because it was me presenting it, but because the topic and the information was exactly why he had come to the conference.

I took this on board and when visiting other clients, I asked them if they had attended the conference and if they remembered me. Some were polite and said, ‘Yes of course,’ while others said they did not remember my presentation at all. When I told them the topic, they said: ‘I don’t deal with that side of the business.’

It made me realise that of the 600 people in the room, only a fraction was interested in the subject I was presenting. It could have been anyone standing in front of them and it would not have mattered.

The fear of standing in front of them was purely of my own making. By thinking about the things that could go wrong, stumbling over my words, answering questions, I had built fear – no one else.

I told my manager about the presentation, and he said he could see that I was nervous and that was understandable. Everyone gets nervous before a presentation – but if you have prepared and organised sufficiently, it will be a success.

I have since given hundreds of presentations. Some have

run smoothly, others have not. Technical issues and external factors can interfere with the best planning, but I learned to have the courage to stand up, present to my fellow colleagues and enjoy the moment.

Is this bravery? Well, standing in front of people is nowhere near the bravery demonstrated by service personnel in the Armed Forces and emergency services who put their lives on the line every day, but it is a form of bravery: the courage to overcome your fears.

One of my colleagues is an amazing woman who is very dedicated to her cause. She interacts with the members of her charity in an amazing way yet when asked to give a presentation, she refused.

After some discussion about the reasons why, she realised she had the same fears I had: what if I stumble over words, the slides do not work, people don't like the speech etc.

I offered to stand with her on the stage when she gave the presentation and she agreed. It was a remarkable success; she had prepared fantastically and was extremely organised. We had rehearsed the presentation to ensure it flowed, and we worked well together.

Before the next conference, we prepared the slides and rehearsed, but she completed it herself. I was close to her but played no part in it at all. It was a fantastic success, extremely well received and was broadcast live across the internet.

The anxiety was still there, but the fear factor had been

reduced after her first presentation. She has since presented to smaller groups with no help and the feedback from the groups is always brilliant.

It does not matter if you are tall, thin, short or fat, the courage comes from within. Steve Jobs was a great presenter. He walked on stage in white trainers, jeans and a sweatshirt and gave the world the iPhone. We do not remember what he was wearing or his hairstyle, but we will remember the iPhone and Steve Jobs forever. His desire and courage to implement a new product drove him forward.

A lot of courage comes from mental strength, the power of the mind to overcome situations. We all have fears (spiders, heights, snakes etc.) but why do we fear presenting or chairing a meeting? For the most part, we know the audience; they are often work colleagues.

Having the courage to confront our problems, or issues that are affecting us every day, can be hard. There may be financial or emotional problems, and the death of a loved one remains with us forever.

But you must never not have the courage to sort out a situation, hiding it away in a drawer, hoping that it will go away. If a situation occurs that you feel you cannot cope with, ask for help or support. Asking for help takes courage and we all need help at some point in our lives.

Courage is a difficult thing to discuss. Many people would rather ignore a problem than embrace it and work through it with help and guidance. We all have feelings that we bottle up inside or hide away from other people. Talking to others about our problems and our fears takes courage.

Listening to other people's problems over many years has led me to believe that everyone has courage; it simply manifests itself in different ways within different people. For some, it is the courage to battle through illness (both mental and physical), struggle with financial constraints or deal with day-to-day life.

We can all help each other as a community. As a group we can support each other. And we all have our own special talents. We all live through the ups and downs of life; some experience more than others and some suffer more than others.

For many years I have been helping a family who have a lot of including physical illness, mental illness, financial issues problems and bereavement. They have battled suicidal thoughts, yet they have the courage to continue; their courage is amazing. Life has not been easy for this family, yet with support they continue to move forward with their lives.

We all have courage, yet we do not realise it. Everyone can stand up and present. And we can help each other. Sometimes it is imposed on us, but other times we can use our inner courage to change lives. Just believe in yourself. Have the courage.

Do You Have the Energy?

The 21st century world is an extremely busy place. On-demand services play a major part in our day to day lives. Pressures of work and family life all drain our energy.

How many times have you arrived home from work exhausted, only to find more jobs requiring your attention?

When was the last time you got over eight hours of unbroken sleep? When was the last time you took time out for yourself?

Our energy levels fluctuate during the day, depending on the tasks we must complete. The importance of eating regularly, getting enough sleep and managing ourselves should not be underestimated.

We have all awoken in the morning, feeling tired from the night before. We may have slept well, but still feel tired. Our energy at the start of the day is low and remains so throughout the day.

The demands placed on us are high. A good work–life balance is difficult to maintain. Our energy must be balanced across the day.

There are numerous studies regarding nutrition and ensuring you maintain a healthy diet, but this must be combined with other factors to ensure we have enough energy throughout the day.

External factors affect our energy. We are only human, and viruses and illnesses affect our energy levels. There will always be factors beyond our control, but we can do our utmost to maintain enough energy to get us through the day.

I attended a course where the lecturer discussed the optimum time for a person to work. Everyone is different: your optimum time may be very early in the morning, or late at night. Our energy levels play a part in this. If we feel tired, we are not working at our optimum level.

We have all attended meetings where, at some point, we have yawned for no reason. It has happened to me during an interactive session which was very interesting, but I still yawned. My energy levels were dropping, and I needed to re-energize myself.

To have drive and enthusiasm is brilliant, but it must be matched with the energy to complete your daily routine. It is natural for a human being to feel tired as we need to regenerate with sleep.

However, we cannot just insert new batteries and immediately recharge ourselves; we must maintain our energy levels and recharge using food, fluid and sleep.

We are all different; we all have different eating habits and tastes. Many people eat on the go, grabbing snacks whilst under pressure. Or we no longer take lunch breaks, or we eat at our desk rather than taking a break to re-energize. We all need to ensure we take breaks, take on regular fluids and food and maintain our energy levels.

As previously stated, everyone is under pressure, but this simple solution – take a break, relax and ensure you take on enough fluid and food – will make a massive difference to your energy levels. Match this with your optimum time for working and your productivity levels will increase dramatically. No one knows your body better than you do, so ensure you have enough energy.

It sounds simple, but it isn't. You need to allocate time to yourself and ensure that you manage this time and do not let other people encroach on it or disrupt it.

When I was 18, I worked on a production line making the plastic telephone boxes that are in everyone's homes. It was a simple line with each member having their own task, some inserting screws, others packing. My colleague had worked on the same production line for over 10 years. The factory was very disciplined: break in the morning, hour lunch break and break in the afternoon, always at the same time.

I found the production line extremely boring and asked him why he had stayed in the same job for so long. He replied: 'I make enough money to support my family, I have no major responsibilities and my working hours are set in stone. No one expects anything else of me apart from making these boxes. I keep my work life separate from my personal life and do not worry about any aspect of my work.'

I immediately thought that this person had no ambition to be promoted, that he lacked drive. But years later, after working in the corporate world and experiencing the demands placed upon me by various companies, I realised he may have been right.

His work–life balance was perfect. He did not take any aspect of his work out of the factory, he was very happy, his energy levels were high because of the regular breaks, he earned enough money, and he enjoyed his work.

We are all different and his attitude to work might not be for you, but if you dissect his approach, we can all learn from him. Regular hours, regular breaks, and enough fluid and food throughout the day maintained his energy levels. He arrived for work on time every day, performed his tasks efficiently and did not cause any issues to his employers.

Do you take the time to sit with your family and eat together? Discuss the day with them, listen to their problems and talk to each other?

Recently I saw a graphic that showed a mobile phone battery at 5%, with the caption ‘You wouldn’t let this happen to your phone, so why let it happen to you?’ It is a brilliant statement. We all feel tired; we are constantly thinking about issues, problems, future appointments and memories.

Having the energy to deal with life can be difficult. When we do take time off from work, or over the Christmas break, we relax and switch off, and generally we feel more tired. You think to yourself, ‘Why am I so tired? I haven’t done anything!’ It is not that you are more tired; it is just your body’s way of telling you to relax and get the required amount of sleep.

Take time to analyse your working day. Record the number of breaks you have and the amount of fluid and food you take in. You may be amazed how little you relax during the day. Many people I have spoken to do not eat breakfast, or skip lunch, then eat a large meal very late at the end of the day.

Energy is desperately important in order to ensure you can carry out the tasks that you want to. We can all prepare, research and get organised, but we must ensure that our energy levels are sufficient to complete the task.

Eating on the run, in the car, skipping meals, not taking in enough fluids, all contribute to low energy levels.

Re-evaluate your day. Include breaks and take time out for yourself and your body. You will feel the effects and your energy levels will rise.

Do You Have Enthusiasm?

Enthusiasm for a task is something most of us have. Some of us enjoy our work and are enthusiastic about the tasks we undertake.

But we all face tasks where we are not enthusiastic. It may be the task seems beyond our capability, or it is a monotonous task that seems boring.

We have all been allocated tasks that we view as being beneath our talents. I personally hate creating reports. Formatting the text and aligning the fields can take a long time to complete, but the final product, when given to a client, is worth the effort.

The colleague that worked on the same production line for over 10 years always had enthusiasm for the job. I asked him how he could be so enthusiastic performing the same role. His response was: 'If I complete my task correctly, these boxes will bring communication to the world. Family and friends will be able to communicate with each other and I helped to make that possible. I may be a small cog in the machine, but without my cog, the machine doesn't work.'

We are all cogs in a machine. Our roles are important, no matter what task we undertake. The job of a cleaner may not seem as important as being the chairman of the board, but if the cleaner does not perform their task, the chairman may not be able to go to the bathroom – a basic requirement for a human being. This may impact a meeting or affect his state of mind or decision-making ability.

I attended a board meeting where the members were complaining that there were no refreshments available. The meeting still went ahead, after they had made their own drinks, but the mood changed and enthusiasm for the meeting was greatly reduced. A simple task we all perform every day became a major talking point.

Was it too much to expect someone to make their own drink? Of course not, but it was expected by the board that refreshments would be available and when they were not, that became the main focus, not the meeting agenda. The meeting was not productive and ended with discussions about the refreshment issue.

A small cog in a larger machine had failed and this had a major effect on the business.

Our enthusiasm is dependent on numerous factors and the tasks we face. We must remember that we are all cogs in a machine that needs to function efficiently. Without the enthusiasm of everyone to complete their task, the machine will not run at its optimum efficiency and may break down.

We all experience tiredness and lack of enthusiasm for basic tasks around the house that form part of our everyday activities, like taking out the rubbish, painting a fence or a wall, tidying up. But we continue to perform the tasks; we ensure that the rubbish is collected, we wash the dishes and clean our clothes.

Whilst we may not think we have enthusiasm for these

tasks, we see them as essential to maintaining our lifestyle – for example, we could not go out if we did not have clean clothes. Are we really enthusiastic or are we just on autopilot, performing the cyclical tasks that are required of us?

I was once asked if I performed tasks around the house like vacuuming, laundry and cleaning. When I replied that I did, the person was shocked. They told me they didn't perform those tasks as 'it wasn't their job'. So I asked them who would do those jobs if they were living on their own and they said they would perform the tasks themselves. So why didn't they do it when living with a partner?

We can all help each other by taking on simple tasks. Your partner may not be looking forward to vacuuming the house, so do it yourself. When they find that a chore they were thinking about has been completed, you will see a smile on their face. It may seem simple, but it will help.

Our enthusiasm is also affected by how we are treated. If we are not appreciated by our manager then we do not complete our tasks with enthusiasm. When he was in charge at Manchester United, Sir Alex Ferguson knew the names of each member of staff and interacted with them, as he understood the value of each employee and their contribution to the smooth running of the club.

We should all appreciate that everyone's role is important and without it, the machine will fail. The board members now appreciate the back-office staff who make their refreshments. In our personal lives, we can all help each other, no matter how small the task; it may be something as simple as a phone call to ask how they are. We can all contribute to someone's enthusiasm.

Many people are not in their ideal job role; they are just working to survive. These people are simply performing the tasks given to them to ensure they receive the financial reward needed to ensure they can pay their bills. Do they have enthusiasm for their role? It is a difficult question to answer, as everyone has different motivations.

I was once told that my enthusiasm during a presentation had influenced someone to take on a new role in which they had been very successful. This was a compliment to me but led me to think about the number of times my lack of enthusiasm may have had the opposite effect on people.

How many times had I complained about a task, influenced my colleagues with my lack of enthusiasm, moaned about my manager "offloading" tasks to me so he could take the credit for himself, only to complete the task and think: 'It wasn't that bad'?

In the company I started, we all cleaned the office, emptied the bins, cleaned the kitchen and the toilet. We still had a management structure and a decision-making tree, but the basic tasks were carried out by everybody. Anyone can clean the kitchen, wash up cups and cutlery and take out the rubbish and just because I was the boss did not mean I should stop performing these tasks. When I was the only employee in the business, I had to do them, so what was different now?

I appreciate that CEOs of large businesses will not be cleaning the toilets but being prepared to do it and showing employees they will do it if necessary is enough to demonstrate that even the smallest cogs are required.

We all have the power to encourage people and raise enthusiasm levels within our community; our enthusiasm rubs off on other people. Be passionate, be enthusiastic and empower others by including them, no matter how small a cog they are.

Someone's enthusiasm for a task should never be underestimated and pride in a task, no matter what the task is, should be rewarded and acknowledged.

How Much Dedication is Needed?

Dedication to a cause is very personal. Some people have an interest in their work, others do not. On a course for not-for-profit organisations, many of the attendees had either set up their organisation or had a personal experience that led them to support the organisation. Others, however, were working for the organisation and using it as a career path. All were equally dedicated to their tasks.

Is dedication to a task a basic requirement, or should it be encouraged? I have taken on tasks where there was a financial reward at the end – did this make me more dedicated to the task? If we can see the task is worthwhile and will make an impact, then we should all be dedicated.

It is very difficult to teach dedication. Take the example of my colleague on the telephone box production line: did he complete his tasks as requested, was he reliable and not disruptive? The answer to all these questions is yes – but was he dedicated to the job?

This is difficult to answer. As far as his employer was concerned, he was a great employee who seemed very dedicated as he was always reliable and punctual. If you asked him, he would say no, he was not dedicated. It was a means to an end to ensure he could live comfortably.

We all have different drivers and levels of dedication. A

priest, for example, is dedicated to a role they believe in; their faith led them to the role. Some people may seem less personally dedicated to a role than others but will ensure that any job is completed to the best of their ability.

One manager I worked under asked a group of us to work a weekend; he asked on the Friday before, and gave us no notice. Several of us already had plans, some had families with young children and others did not want the extra work. There was a financial incentive, but only one person – a middle-aged man with no commitments – took up the offer.

The manager praised the volunteer and then accused the other employees of not being dedicated to the company because we had not volunteered. Was this a lack of dedication to the company – or poor planning and organisation? Unfortunately, this accusation caused a rift between the employees and the manager, which was never healed.

We need to appreciate that people have personal lives and commitments outside the workplace, which we may or may not know about, that impact on how much time they can dedicate to their work commitments.

Many people have other commitments and these can be very personal and may be health related. This can have a major impact on their dedication to the tasks they are allocated and we need to understand the individual issues that people are living with every day.

One of my colleagues told me he really needed the extra work and the extra money, but because he had young children, he could not commit to it. His dedication to his job was not in question; his commitments to his family meant he was unable to take up the offer.

If we run our own business, then our dedication levels increase. The number of hours we work to make the business a success and the time taken away from family commitments increases, and this affects our work–life balance. We all need to sleep, eat and relax our minds in order to function efficiently, and dedication can play a major part in upsetting this balance.

Next time you question someone's dedication, consider the other commitments they may have. Missing a child's school play or football match might not be important to some, but for others it is desperately important as these moments cannot be replayed: they are one-offs that need to be experienced.

'I can't do it…'

The sentence 'I can't do it' is one I hear every time I present to an audience. And remember, I once thought I could not stand in front of people and give a talk.

We all have different personalities: some people are outgoing, others reserved. There are several factors that affect people's ability to present or express opinions.

Experiences of bad management can lead to employees not engaging with projects and not making themselves heard. My father always told me if I had an opinion, I should voice it; if I left a meeting complaining that my views weren't heard, it was my fault.

This philosophy is something I have stuck to. I will voice my opinion and if it leads to further debate or discussion then so be it.

I worked with a female colleague who had a soft voice. The management did not involve her in any decision making; she attended the meetings but did not contribute. She understood the issues and did have her own opinion but was never asked for it. When I took over chairing the meetings, I asked for her thoughts on a topic. The other participants groaned, and she declined to give her opinion.

After the meeting, I asked a few participants why they had groaned. Their response shocked me. 'If you ask her opinion, she never gives it. She never communicates very well.'

Before the next meeting, I asked her to present an agenda item. Her response was that she could not do it. I insisted and gave her time in her schedule to prepare a presentation.

At the meeting, the other participants were shocked when I announced that she was going to present the agenda item, and again there were groans. I had not given her any guidance, yet her presentation was extremely well put together, it was factually correct, and she ensured that everyone heard her point.

Discussions regarding the agenda item were then undertaken. I asked everyone to put their questions to her, not to me, and she answered each one professionally, proving that she had completed her research.

The other participants were shocked to realise she was a good communicator and dedicated to her tasks. She did have a voice. She just needed the right stage to be heard.

Preparing the right stage for people to come forward and be heard is difficult. For some, they have no problem with getting up on any stage; for others, they would rather sit at the back of the room and not participate. By empowering them, looking at their strengths and weaknesses and working with them, you can ensure they have input into the organisation.

I worked with a fantastic programmer who would write incredible source code, but once you gave him a task, you left him alone to complete it; he was not a 'people' person and did not like to be disturbed whilst working on a project. He immersed himself in the task and ensured it was completed on time, every time. He never said, 'I can't do it.' He would give you a time frame for the work and deliver it on time, if he was not disturbed.

While he was working on a project, a director was giving a tour of the building to a prospective client. I was introduced as project leader and he then turned to my colleague. We all knew he did not like to be disturbed and meeting a prospective client was not something he would want to do.

When the director came to his desk, he told him to go away, but not so politely. The director was outraged. He apologised to the prospective client, quickly ushered him from the room and then returned without the client 15 minutes later.

He immediately started shouting at my colleague, who calmly told him: 'You gave me a task to complete this code today. If I waste time meeting prospective clients, I will not complete it. Which is more important?'

The director replied that the prospective client was due to sign a contract potentially worth hundreds of thousands of pounds. My colleague replied, 'Doesn't affect my work. You have already put me behind, and this conversation is putting me behind even further. Now go away and let me finish what I committed to do.'

Instead of arguing, the director turned and left the room. My colleague calmly sat down and continued his source code development. He did not complain; he just carried on as if nothing had happened.

As his direct line manager, I was called to the director's office. He was incensed; he was extremely angry. I was told to discipline the programmer. I refused.

My colleague was the best programmer we had. He was efficient and always completed on time; he was never late for work and he was extremely dedicated.

Other directors got involved. The situation was getting out of hand, until the chairman of the board entered the room and asked what the problem was. He then asked one simple question of the director. 'Meeting clients is not in his job description. He has had no training or guidance on this. How can you expect him to deal with this situation without the correct preparation?'

Immediately the room fell silent. The chairman then said, 'Leave him to perform the duties he has done for several years. He is the best programmer we have.'

The situation was not that the programmer could not do it, but rather that he did not want to do it. He was immersed in his own job role and surprising him with a client visit had upset his routine, leaving him feeling that he would not be able to complete the task he had committed to. He was not interested in the director's tasks, just his own.

Everyone has their own 'I can't do it' moment; it may be personal or in a work environment. Speaking in front of an audience is one shared by many people. But with coaching, empowerment and active listening, people can overcome their fears and they can do it.

Ensure that you work with people, stand with them, encourage them, help them and, most of all, believe in them. Talk to your inner circle of friends and family, help them in small ways, show that you care, listen to their issues and their problems and help them.

You will be surprised at the outcome.

Pressure

We all feel pressure, to varying degrees. We are often put into situations where pressure is applied to us that makes us feel uncomfortable.

People deal with pressure in different ways. Some cope with pressure extremely well, while others do not cope at all. Unfortunately, pressure can lead to suicide; there are too many cases where the pressure of life has led to the ultimate sacrifice.

Expectations of us are high. Some parents put pressure on their children to perform well at school, at sports or in music or drama. Each of us is different.

With management comes pressure. Management can be personal; it can include management of finances, children, a house, a car. All are pressures we feel every day. Some people are lucky and do not feel the financial pressures, but most of us must work to pay our bills.

Work pressure is predominately applied by our managers, but we also put pressure on ourselves. Taking on tasks with impossible deadlines is one example.

Our skills are more in demand than ever before. We must look for these pressure points and reduce them as much as possible. Sharing the load as a collective group is one way to ensure that no member of the team is overloaded. Discussing workloads within the team and assigning realistic deadlines is another.

In the case of my colleague who immersed himself in his work, he always worked under his own pressure: he made the deadlines and worked to them. If you tried to give him an unrealistic deadline, he would tell you it was not possible and would offer an alternative. Unfortunately, some people will take the impossible deadline and then try to work towards it. This usually ends in failure. Making impossible deadlines is down to poor management; someone must have made the decision to impose the deadline. It is up to the person who is completing the work or has responsibility for the work to tell them that it is impossible.

Unfortunately, many projects fail because of unrealistic deadlines. I was working on a new system for fundraising when the sales team came to see my manager and me and told us they had sold an add-on to the system which would enable quick, rapid entry of data. This module did not exist and had not been specified, yet the sales team had promised it to complete the sale.

The first question my manager asked was: 'What is the deadline?' It was due to be presented in 72 hours. It was impossible to have a working version in that timeframe. Arguments regarding the stupidity of the sales team led to directors getting involved. I was invited to the meeting and asked if I could meet the deadline with the new add-on. I said it was impossible.

I was then asked what was possible. Bearing in mind that I already had a number of projects scheduled for the next few weeks and I did not have any spare time, my response was, 'Nothing. We have no capacity without dropping other projects.'

Discussions regarding the contract and the amount of money it would generate for the company were then undertaken, within my hearing.

I was then asked: if I had a clear 72 hours, how much could I achieve? I told them it would be possible to show a prototype to the client, but most of the functionality would not be working, it would simply be a demonstration. We would also need a full specification before proceeding.

This was agreed by the sales team and directors and my manager, who put my other projects back by 72 hours.

After the meeting, my manager told me not to work outside of the normal hours of business on this project, and to deliver what we promised and nothing more.

I cleared my diary and worked on the project from home, where I had no work distractions. Because I was under pressure to deliver the prototype, I did work longer than my normal business hours to ensure it was ready to demonstrate to the client.

I delivered it on time to the sales team, who then informed me that I would be travelling with them and I was to present the prototype. This was not part of the task that I had agreed, but my manager had agreed to it in my absence, which I was not happy about.

I presented the prototype. It was bought by the client, developed in a timely manner and then sold to every client as an add-on to the existing systems, bringing in extra revenue for the company.

This pressure to deliver was at the time a major issue for me. I had to refocus, re-order my diary and deliver what I promised. Now that I own a business and employ developers, I never impose unrealistic deadlines on the team. We discuss the tasks and ensure that everyone is meeting their deadlines and is not under any extra pressure other than what they have committed to themselves.

When allocating tasks, we must allow for external factors to affect deadlines. Extra pressure in our personal lives, such as illness or family commitments, plays a part in the ability to deliver a task.

By including extra time in a task, it can be delivered on time or before the deadline.

My manager told me that if I was late for a meeting, I was to apologise, but not to blame traffic. Everyone knows that the roads can be congested – so don't use it as an excuse. Instead, next time make time to plan your journey, allowing for delays and unforeseen circumstances. We all experience traffic, car failure, illness and other external factors that influence our day. These are all extra pressure applied to us.

How we handle pressure depends on us. We can help people deal with pressure by ensuring that impossible deadlines are not imposed on them. Being understanding of illness and ensuring there is enough time in the plan for unforeseen circumstances is key to ensuring that pressure does not build up.

If you are feeling pressure at work, speak to your manager and let them know how you feel. It is not a failure to say, 'I cannot cope.' Do not suffer in silence. Do not wait until the last minute to tell your manager that you are not going to meet the deadline. Tell them in advance, so extra resources or an extension can be sought to relieve the pressure.

Think of the number of times that you bring your work home with you and how it affects your home life. It is difficult to separate the two, but if you use the steps in this book, you can stop and think about situations and how they are affecting your life.

You are not a failure if you do not meet an unrealistic deadline. Do not accept any task that you are pressurized into taking. If you know you cannot meet the deadline when it is assigned, say so; do not take on an impossible task.

It is not a weakness to say 'No.' It is a sign of strength. We can control the pressure put on us from different sources. Through honest, clear communication, the pressure can be relieved.

We all have pressures in our personal life, especially when struggling with finances, but they can be overcome using the Halt 2 Proceed steps.

We must never feel that the pressure is too much for us to handle because we are never alone. Some people do not communicate their problems or the pressure they are facing and they bottle it up inside. You must remember to always communicate with people. There are so many options available to you.

Pressure can be relieved in many ways. Discussing issues with other people can be extremely beneficial, as can researching the options, and joining online forums with like-minded people will show you that you are not alone. Many people have experienced the pressures you may be feeling now and have dealt with them and will be willing to help you. Use your time to research support groups and reach out. Sharing a problem and discussing it with friends, colleagues or within like-minded groups will relieve the pressure.

When a pressure cooker is under pressure, you lift the lid to release it. Apply this principle to your life pressures. Lift the lid.

Experience

I was once told by my manager, 'There is no substitute for experience,' but as a young programmer, how was I to get the experience if I was not given the chance? I was lucky: he gave me experience by including me in meetings and having enough belief in me to allocate projects to me.

Unfortunately, not everyone is so lucky. However, we all have experiences – some good, some bad – and we must reflect on these experiences and learn from them.

Everyone has heard the saying 'You learn something new every day.' This is true, but you also experience new things every day. You are put in situations that you have not encountered before; you must deal with conflict and resolution.

As you move along your career path, generally the responsibilities increase. I worked at a company whose managers were promoted on the basis of being the longest serving employees. They were not the best managers, and many did not want the position, but the financial reward was so high that they accepted the position.

Being a good manager, making sure tasks are completed and managing a team is difficult. When dealing with different personalities, ages and genders, you often rely on your experience to get you through situations.

But we can usually learn from experience. For example, as

children we learn that a fire will burn us, and this experience ensures that we do not burn ourselves as adults. We learnt from that experience.

My immediate manager would not employ recently graduated students unless they had taken a gap year and worked in the 'real world', as he called it. He needed programmers who could integrate within a team and fit in immediately. Yet he took on students for their gap year and ensured that they gained experience. I was one of two students who he gave this opportunity to and both of us went back to work for the company.

I learnt more in the gap year with him and the team than I did in my two years at university. It is hard to be a new employee, especially when you are only 19. But with help and guidance from the other members of the team I learnt a lot and experienced what was needed to succeed.

We all have bad experiences and need to take time to analyse them and learn from it. It may be a situation we would not put ourselves in again; it may be a task we took on, knowing it was impossible.

Now that I have 30 years' experience, I look back at the memory of my gap year and realise I was so inexperienced. I knew nothing about the running of a company and the pressures that the directors were facing every day. My manager was under intense pressure to deliver his projects.

It was only when the company made redundancies that I realised the pressures of running a successful company are enormous. To make the decision to make people redundant is one I have never had to do but choosing staff must be the hardest choice possible.

I have taken these experiences and applied them to my companies. When you manage people, situations arise that must be resolved. Some of these situations are difficult to manage, but if you successfully negotiate the situation and learn from the experience, then you can evolve as a person.

I once experienced a manager who micro-managed the team. He wanted to know everything that was happening, especially on the financial side. He imposed regular checks on all spending and any requests for stationery, including a single pen, had to be approved by him.

He introduced individual codes for the photocopier, so he could manage the amount of copying that each person was doing. This led to the team rebelling against him. One member of the team asked the photocopier engineer for the list of the codes and then told everyone the manager's code. We all used it for the next month and at the end of the month, when he analysed the photocopier log, all the printing was against his name.

He had imposed rules without discussing them with the team and the team soon let him know that they were not happy. He turned off the codes and learned from his mistake.

The team had spoken against him as a collective and he understood that he had made a mistake and needed to engage with the team first. He was trying to impose his authority as a manager, but soon lost the respect of his team.

His style of management changed over the next few months and the team progressed, worked well together and achieved the projects they had been allocated.

Unfortunately, not everyone learns from experience. 'It is my way or the highway!' is one saying I have heard. Even if the manager's way is not the correct one, they are unwilling to listen to the team and will not concede in any way. This style of management often leads to high staff turnover. Usually the manager remains and their staff change, when in fact the manager needs to change or be trained in people management.

It is difficult to confront a manager or to challenge them, but by working collectively as a team and ensuring that everyone involved is included and informed, the team will be far more productive, and the working environment will be a happy one. Informed, happy employees with realistic tasks will work more efficiently than stressed, unhappy, overworked employees.

Life experiences allow us to grow as a person. We may experience personal problems, disappointments and bereavements that affect us in many ways. Many of us experiment with things, for example, alcohol and dangerous relationships. We also experience happy moments in our lives: loving relationships, children, financial rewards and happy memories.

Our experiences shape who we are and most people learn from them. Use your experiences, both good and bad. They are what make you the person you are now. We have all experience, and you can utilise it to your advantage.

Communication

How well do you communicate with your friends, family and colleagues? Communication is key to ensuring that everyone is aware of what is required of them and that they are working as a team.

Obviously, not everyone in a company needs to know what is going on at each level, but if someone is involved in a project or a team, they should be included, no matter what their role. At the company I worked for, we had a weekly departmental meeting to ensure that the whole department knew what was being planned for the week. This included the development department, engineers, and the sales team. This meeting was only scheduled for an hour, but it enabled everyone to understand the pressures felt by the different teams within the department.

New projects, existing projects, timeframes and issues were all discussed, and plans put in place to address any concerns. Everyone had an opportunity to have input in the meeting and raise any problems.

This approach to the department ensured that everyone had an insight into the workings of the different teams. They did not have detailed plans from each section, just an overview. This led to the team understanding each other's pressures and enabled the team to work together, swapping resources where necessary.

We can utilise this in our own private lives when

communicating with our family and friends. Sharing issues and communicating our problems releases pressure, stress and anxiety.

Utilising community groups, charities and associations who share a common bond is an excellent way to communicate with your peers. There are many organisations across the world who share your beliefs and many people are experiencing the same issues as you. These people can help, so reach out and communicate with them.

But can we have too much communication? As a manager, I found myself spending most of my day in meetings. In some of the meetings, I did not even participate in any of the discussions. It was a waste of my time, which would have been better spent with my team. Balancing communication is a difficult task: too little, and people are not informed; too much, and the efficiency of the team is impacted.

Digital communication has helped us to ensure that remote workers are kept in touch with projects and the team. Video calling, instant messaging and collaborative working tools allow for everyone to be involved.

Cloud storage and team working is now commonplace and with the tools on offer, we can ensure that communication is kept to the minimum required for efficient working but is enough to ensure that everyone is informed.

But do you allow the team to communicate? Is the communication always dictated from the top? In an efficient working environment, the team should communicate with each other, give updates on projects, provide encouragement, help each other, and ensure that the help they require is available.

One such example is a forum, where people who have never met exchange experiences and help other people with issues. People are willing to help strangers with problems, especially if they have faced them before and found a solution.

We should all try and help each other. If you are experiencing problems with a deadline or are facing any issue, communicate with the team and ask for help. Problems can be solved quickly and easily.

I experienced this after working on an issue for several hours with a program that would not function correctly. I was tearing my hair out. Eventually I reached out to a colleague of mine who was not working on my project, but he had worked with the software I was using, and I believed he may have the answer.

Within five minutes, he replied and told me to tick a box on a specific option and it would be solved. It worked! He then told me he had spent the same amount of time figuring it out and another colleague had given him the solution, which he was happy to pass on.

I may have figured it out, but the hours my colleague saved me was amazing. The project was finished early and he saved me a lot of time, let alone relieving the frustration caused by the issue. He communicated his experience to me, and I have since passed this on to another programmer.

Some people are terrible at communicating. They feel as if they are failures if they ask for help. This is not the case. Asking friends, family members and work colleagues for help and communicating problems, issues and achievements should be encouraged.

If a project is finished early or an application for funds accepted, or they ensured that a problem was resolved, congratulate the person – in fact, encourage the whole team to congratulate them. The positivity of communication is one which should not be underestimated.

Receiving a compliment on work issues, even if it is a passing remark, is an action that encourages people and makes them feel happy. Encouragement from a director or board member is especially important. My managing director made sure he knew everyone in the company, over 125 employees at one stage. He often stopped and asked how things were progressing, how you felt and to remind you that he was available to talk to at any time.

This level of interaction is incredible from someone who was under extreme pressure to run a multi-million-pound company and deliver to the shareholders. Receiving a compliment from him was a boost to anyone. You felt energized and, more importantly, a valued employee.

If you find it difficult to communicate, take time to analyse how you do it. Look at the channels you currently use and explore new ones. But, most importantly, ask your family, friends and colleagues; involve them in the communication process. Ask their opinion on the current channels and how they can be improved.

It saddens me when I read articles about suicide and the last hours of those people who have taken their own lives. In many cases they feel as if they have no one to talk to, no one to communicate with.

There is so much help available to everyone, so much support from many networks, you just need to ask. Please do not suffer in silence. Communicate with the many people who will help you.

If you are struggling at work, communicate with your manager, the directors or HR department. People will help you if you reach out to them.

Solitude

The act of self-reflection and solitude – taking time to reflect on the day, on your own, with no external influences – is underused by everyone.

When was the last time you spent time on your own, relaxing and reflecting, analysing your day and looking at the decisions you made?

It is usually only when a catastrophic event happens that we take time to reflect and, with hindsight, wish we had done things differently. It may be the death of a loved one, being made redundant, moving to a new house or a relationship breakdown. These all make us re-evaluate our lives.

Taking time to look back and evaluate is something we should make time to do every day.

Whenever I discuss solitude with people, they always tell me they do not have time: 'I never get a minute to myself.' For some people, this is true; a busy home life with children, working full time and being pressured by managers to take on impossible tasks, working longer hours, and working at home all have a part to play.

Within the Halt 2 Proceed programme, we use an 'allotment of life'. This is a drawing of the current time spent during the day on different tasks. At the end of the programme, we ask the participants to draw an ideal allotment of life and then challenge them to achieve this. Ninety-five per cent of people fail to include time for self-reflection and solitude.

By allocating time for this, both at work and at home, the change in the work–life balance is amazing. I can testify to this. I was spending ridiculous amounts of time on work and charity business until I attended the Clore Social Leadership course. As part of the course, I was coached by Pat Joseph and we set targets for reducing the amount of work I completed, and allocated time to personal tasks (such as football training and matches with my son). We made everyone aware that I was unavailable during those times.

At first, I was sceptical. I already had too much on my to-do list, so reducing the amount of time I spent on these tasks seemed a step in the wrong direction. However, by delegating some tasks to other members of the team and trusting them, and taking time out and reflecting on the day, my to-do list has reduced dramatically, and time spent with my family has increased. Productivity has also increased and I have achieved many goals that seemed impossible.

At work, simply by stopping, analysing the work–life balance, looking at areas that can be delegated, making time for personal life, being disciplined and not working crazy hours, the teams are working more efficiently too.

Solitude and self-reflection can be achieved in different ways. For some, this might mean a soak in a warm bath, with candles and soothing music. For others it's taking a walk. Every one of us is different and achieves solitude in different ways. Give yourself 15 minutes a day in your diary to self-reflect and take yourself away from day to day life with no interruptions. It is possible! Most importantly, ensure that everyone in your life is aware of this time and that it is important to you.

We now have more time at home due to the pandemic, but this does not mean that the demands on our time are any less; in fact, the opposite is often true. Home schooling children, ensuring they have the technology, looking after loved ones or fighting the pandemic as an essential worker, the tension and anxiety caused by the pandemic adds to our daily stress.

Solitude is now more important than ever. Taking time for ourselves, watching a favourite programme, reading a book, going for a walk, exercising, or taking a bath are all activities that can help us to relax and take solitude.

We can all self-reflect on decisions we have made, how the day went, how we would have done things differently. Take the time today.

Do You Have a Gift to Give?

I ordered a book that had changed the way I thought to give to a colleague as a surprise. It was not expensive, we had discussed it in a coaching session, and I thought it would help her. She was overwhelmed by the gesture. She read it and it changed her way of thinking as well. She said the gift was a wonderful gesture and she would pass on the book to others.

We all have a gift to give. This may be time, wisdom or physical gifts.

Making a difference to someone's life does not need to impact on our lives as much as we think it will. I always refer to the story of a man whose friends supported him financially. One gave him £50 and the other £500. He thanked them both but appreciated the £50 more because the person who gave him the £500 had hundreds of thousands of pounds in spare cash, whereas the person who gave him £50 only had £100 spare; he had given him 50% of his spare cash.

We can all help others, through our knowledge and experience, but most importantly by listening and giving our time. Time is the most precious commodity we possess. We are all time limited and we do not know when our time will run out.

Making time to help a colleague or even a stranger on a forum could change their world by saving them time or helping them through a problem. We all have a gift to give, no matter how small.

Action learning sets provide a group of people with the opportunity to help a member of the group, by acting out a scenario and asking questions about their issue and then acting out the situation within the group. These action learning sets are a fantastic tool for solving issues and provide a chance for the team to interact with each other.

Taking time to listen to and understand your family, friends and work colleagues will be beneficial, as is giving a small gift to a person, such as allowing them to leave work early or work from home. These gifts can make a big difference.

You might hope that the person will repay you for your gifts when they are needed to perform extra tasks or when you next need help. But this is not the reason to give a gift; the reason is to make a difference. We feel better when we give.

Gifts given and exchanged can enhance the interaction between people. Experienced team members can help less experienced colleagues by sharing knowledge and insights into problems they have encountered and how to overcome them. Swapping a shift on a work rota to enable a colleague to be with their family ensures that the work ethic between team members is enhanced.

Encourage the exchange of gifts; everyone has a gift to give. The gift does not have to be a huge bonus or a major item. Even the smallest gift can make a big difference to the person receiving it. Next time you can give a gift, do it.

Fighting the Storm

There are days when everything seems impossible. Tasks get on top of us, our energy levels dip, we become angry and tense, and we forget to take solitude and do not take a step back and relax.

We feel as if we are a fighting a storm. It is a battle we are going to lose, but we should not let the stress of a bad day distract us from our goals.

Remembering the Halt 2 Proceed programme, we can at any time stop and use the tools available to us, by analysing the issue, taking a step back and looking at the situation facing us. Although at times we will face problems with no solution (such as illness and death), most issues are not major problems. My grandmother would always sit me down when I was facing an issue and say, 'Did anyone die?' When I said 'No,' she replied, 'It isn't that bad then, is it?'

Problems we see as insurmountable are often, when analysed, not major issues and with the help of our team, they can be resolved. How many times have you faced a problem, got extremely stressed and worried about it, only to find it was not as challenging as you first thought?

Separating personal problems and work problems is difficult. One manager told me to leave my personal life at home and not bring it to work. But is this possible? If you have a sick child at home, will you be productive that day at work? Will they be on your mind throughout the day? Of course they will; it is human nature.

We must all prioritise the things in our life, and work is not our top priority. Our family and children will always take priority, as well as our health. Yet we struggle to work when we are feeling ill because we need the financial gain. We work throughout the day, just attending without being productive, so we can take home a pay check at the end of the month.

When we do not feel well, or are struggling with personal issues, do we discuss them with our manager? Are they approachable? As a manager, are you approachable?

Would you recognise when a team member is not feeling well or is not performing to the best of their ability? Do you understand their issues? How would you manage the situation? Have you prepared yourself as a manager for this situation?

If you are facing difficulties, you are fighting the storm. How do you handle yourself? Do you hide the problem from your family, friends, and work colleagues, or do you explain it to them?

How you handle the situation depends on the make-up of your team and how you are managing them, how well you know them and how well they know you.

You must remember, however, that at some point we are all fighting the storm. Everyone has good days and bad days, and we must ensure that everyone is fully supported and the goals set for the day are analysed and, if necessary, adjusted.

Do not underestimate the impact that one person's personal issues can have on a situation; everyone can be affected.

Many people are always fighting a storm yet they hide their problems and issues and still smile. When asked about their problems, they say 'I am okay.

We are all human; we are all affected by the world around us. The 'noise' of the world has an impact on us. We do not know what we will face daily; we will have good days and bad days.

We all experience sadness and happiness. We are all fighting the storm. How we handle situations depends on many factors, but if you can use the Halt 2 Proceed principles, you can fight the storm and battle through it.

How Can I Do It?

Now that you have read this book, you are either saying 'I can do that?' or 'How can I do it?' It seems as if it is impossible to just stop, take stock of our lives, change key aspects and then plan out the future. But you have already gone through this process several times, from deciding which subjects to study at school and which vocation to follow, to relationships, when to get married, have children etc.

I read an article entitled 'I have tried adulthood, I don't like it, I want to be a child again.' The article was a detailed look at the responsibilities of being an adult as opposed to being a child, where we have no financial burdens or work pressures. However, when looking at the pressures felt as a child from school, friends and parents, they are still evident, just in a different form.

We have all made decisions we later regret – not investing in a certain stock option, breaking up a relationship, changing jobs. But there are many that we do not regret, and they can be the reverse. Not investing in a stock option that subsequently crashes is a positive decision.

We all have different financial burdens, different personal responsibilities and work commitments, but we can manage them all in the same way. Taking time to stop and look at where you are in life and where you want to be, using self-reflection and the techniques within this book can be extremely beneficial.

They do not have to be radical steps and they do not have to be taken all in one go. Concentrate on the main aspects of your life that you want to change and how you will implement the change. It may be a change of career or job role within an organisation, a change of location, working fewer hours, or a change in your responsibilities.

You may want to do more with your career, return to education or change direction completely. Discuss the options with your family, friends and work colleagues, look at the career opportunities, look at your home life and the work–life balance. If you want to step back and undertake less work, look at the financial aspects of the change and plan for it.

We obviously cannot plan for the unexpected. Changes happen in our lives without warning. We lose loved ones, we get sick, we lose jobs – these are things that are beyond our control and we must deal with them as they arise.

During the COVID pandemic, it is even more important to look after yourself. You would not let your phone battery run down without charging it, and you need to take this approach with yourself. A fully charged you is much more productive than a drained you.

You can do it. You can change your life for the better by taking the time now to halt and proceed as you wish.

Bring People Back to Themselves

I once undertook a presentation to a board of trustees. I was questioned thoroughly by one trustee, who happened to be a billionaire. I asked her what the secret of her success was, and she told me: 'I got lucky.'

She had not worked any harder than anyone else. The idea she had been working on became a massive success and she sold the business for billions of dollars and retired. She then gave her time to charities across the world, advising them and giving them her knowledge, as well as donating money.

She could purchase anything she wanted, did not need to work or give up her time, but she had changed the direction of her life and wanted to give back to society.

This might seem easy for a billionaire, but the demands on her time and finances were so enormous that she still employed a team of people to deal with her affairs. She decided what she was going to achieve and who to give her time and money to.

We can all do this. Time is the most precious commodity in the world. Giving up your time to help someone is an amazing thing that more people should do, but balancing your time across your commitments is something everyone should do.

I ask people, if you won the lottery, what would you do? Buy a fast car, big house, take a world cruise? But what about the later years – does boredom set in? Several lottery winners have returned to work because they needed to balance their lives again.

Looking at ourselves and where we are, what we want to achieve, what our problems are, how we are going to solve them is not an easy task, but it is achievable.

Think back to when you had just left school, college, or university. What did you want to achieve? We all have different ambitions. For some, having a family is their main goal. Others strive to earn enormous amounts of money. We are all driven by our desires and we should return to those initial desires and look at what we have achieved. If we have not achieved them, is it a bad thing? Did our lives take a different path? Are we content with what we have?

For some, the answer to the contentment question is yes, and there is no problem with this. There are many unfortunate people in this world who do not have food to eat, so we should always look upon our own lives and be thankful for what we have. Most of all, we need to be happy. Take time to do the fun stuff, the things you enjoy. 'I don't have time' is no excuse. We can all make time to ensure we have the correct balance in our lives.

Cars, sport, music, clothes – we all have a passion for something. When did you last spend time on that passion? If your work–life balance is so out of kilter you are spending so much time at work that you no longer have time for your passion, you need to re-evaluate.

Remember, time is precious. We do not know what is around the corner. Enjoy life and look after yourself.

I was told by a company director that no one was irreplaceable within the workplace; companies move on, the people change. This is true of any working environment – if you were unable to work for any reason, the company would hire someone else to take your place.

But within your family environment, you are irreplaceable; you can never be replaced. Think of the times you have missed family gatherings, or occasions such as weddings or birthdays. These events will never happen again. I have a DVD of a family gathering from over 30 years ago, when I was a 15-year-old teenager. It is the only video we have of everyone together. It never happened again – people have died, and they can never be replaced.

Take the time and spend it with family and loved ones. If you can't see them in person, make a video call or pick up the telephone. There are many of us who would like to hear a loved one's voice and cannot; we are never that busy.

Technology has allowed us to be together when we are far apart. Use it! You will make someone's day by speaking to them.

I hate the saying 'The telephone works both ways.' It is true, but make the first move. Text them or call them and ask how they are doing. You will be amazed by the outcome.

Conclusion

Taking time for ourselves and understanding others sounds simple. It isn't. It takes dedication and effort. Making the decision to halt our very busy lives and evaluate where we are and where we want to go is a difficult step to take, but it will be worth it.

Follow the Halt 2 Proceed programme in all areas of your life. It will change your life. Adjusting your work–life balance and empowering others will prepare you for the challenges ahead.

There are always surprises in our lives, some good, others bad, but we need to work through them and learn from them. The ability to always be well prepared and having the courage to see our tasks through is in all of us.

Ensuring you are heard and allowing others within your circle to be heard is essential. Allow your family, friends and work colleagues to have a voice and ensure they hear your voice when it is necessary to do so.

Everyone has a different personality and interacts in different ways. Knowing your team and ensuring they interact in the most efficient way takes time, but it is worth the effort. Your team will become more productive and you will be less stressed.

Differentiating between work and personal life and ensuring that the boundaries are not blurred can be achieved. You can turn off the mobile phone alerts, you can ignore emails and you can enforce times when you are dedicating yourself to your personal life.

Before mobile communication and the internet, our work lives were more clearly defined. Once we left our workplace, we were not contactable; we had no communication. This can be achieved by establishing the rules within your inner circle. Everyone needs to recharge at some point. Our busy lives take a toll on our bodies and our wellbeing.

Ensuring that our bodies are charged and ready for the challenges ahead is a challenge that we must overcome. Making time for ourselves with solitude and self-reflection is a step we must all take to ensure we are prepared. We have time in our schedules, or we can make time by delegating and empowering team members.

Do not underestimate the change that this programme can make on your life. You can do it. Halt, evaluate and then proceed on a new path. You will not look back.

Summary

Always remember the 11 steps to Halt 2 Proceed:

H – Hearsay

A – Assumptions

L – Listening

T – Thinking

P – Preparation

R – Research

O – Organisation

C – Courage

E – Energy

E – Enthusiasm

D – Dedication

Use these steps every day and take the time for solitude and self-reflection. Even small changes to our lives can be extremely beneficial, not only to ourselves, but also to those around us, with whom we interact every day.

Remember that you do have time to HALT. You are in control and you must look after yourself and your wellbeing so you can PROCEED.

The Halt 2 Proceed Programme

If, after reading this book, you would like to find out more about Halt 2 Proceed, and maybe even implement the training programme in your business, visit the Motiv8 and Inspir8 website: www.motiv8andinspir8.guru where you will find full details of the available programmes.

The Halt 2 Proceed programme is a unique workshop that enables people to look into themselves, their characteristics and how they interact with others.

This workshop will allow people to communicate effectively; it teaches a new way of interacting with others. A full online version is now available, which you can subscribe to, so you can return to individual steps and continue along your journey.

During the workshop, Alan Owen, author of *Halt 2 Proceed*, takes people on a journey of discovery and self-reflection which will analyse their environment and work–life balance.

The workshop is a must for anyone of any experience, no matter what their situation.

Sessions can be held on or off-site, at locations across the UK. It is often beneficial to interact with other people to gain insight into the issues they face and how they deal with them.

For further information, please visit the website www.motiv8andinspir8.guru or call 0845 075 8175 and a member of the team will help you.

About the Author

Alan Owen is from an IT background, working in the software development sector. After leaving college, he worked as a Unix programmer before starting his own company in 1994, aged 23.

Retiring in 2001 to take on a consultancy role, he spent six years as a consultant before taking over his original company in 2007. ICARIS is now the market leader in beneficiary systems in the UK.

In 2014 he became a fellow of the British Computer Society (BCS) and in 2016 achieved Chartered IT Professional (CITP) Status and is now a CITP assessor for the BCS.

He was also Chairman of the British Nuclear Test Veterans Association (BNTVA), taking over in 2016 until 2020 and driving the UK charity forward, increasing their social media and online presence by over 16,000% to over one million post reach in 2018. Alan's father, who served in the Royal Navy, was a nuclear test veteran.

In 2018, Alan became a GDPR Practitioner, providing training and seminars on implementing GDPR.

In 2019, he graduated as a Clore Leadership fellow, following his participation in the nine-month Clore Emerging Leader course.

In 2020, he founded LABRATS International, which has brought the Atomic Community together across the world.

Alan has provided training and talks to thousands of people across the world and he has spoken at the National Association of Atomic Veterans' annual conference in the USA for three consecutive years.

His interactive style and ability to engage an audience has developed into the Halt 2 Proceed interactive workshops and presentations. His experience and desire to improve the way people interact with each other is at the heart of the programme.

Alan is married with one son and lives in Carmarthen, South Wales. He has a passion for fast cars and is undertaking a Master's Degree.

www.ingramcontent.com/pod-product-compliance
Ingram Content Group UK Ltd.
Pitfield, Milton Keynes, MK11 3LW, UK
UKHW021050270726
13967UKWH00012B/195

9 781916 331402